Printable Piano Accompaniments

PLAYBACK+
Speed · Pitch · Balance · Loop

CONTENTS

To access recordings and PDF piano accompaniments, go to:
www.halleonard.com/mylibrary

Enter Code
5916-0825-5437-5229

ISBN 978-1-4803-5242-1

RUBANK®

HAL•LEONARD®
7777 W. BLUEMOUND RD. P.O. BOX 13819 MILWAUKEE, WI 53213

Visit Hal Leonard Online at
www.halleonard.com

Pavane pour une Infante Défunte

1st B♭ Clarinet (Solo)

Maurice Ravel
Arranged by Harold L. Walters

Pavane pour une Infante Défunte

2nd B♭ Clarinet (Duet)

Maurice Ravel
Arranged by Harold L. Walters

00121405

Two Russian Pieces

B♭ Clarinet

I – Lament

Vasily Kalinikov
Transcribed by H. Voxman

* Add top side key to play B.

II – Patrol Russe

Victor Voloshinov
Transcribed by H. Voxman

Marche Comique

Bb Clarinet

Leroy Ostransky

Adoration

B♭ Clarinet

Felix Borowski
Arranged by Clair W. Johnson

Largo and Allegro
from Sonata I, Op. 3

B♭ Clarinet

Jean-Baptiste Loeillet
Transcribed by H. Voxman
Continuo by R. Hervig

00121405

Russian Sailors' Dance

from *The Red Poppy*

B♭ Clarinet

Reinhold Glière
Arranged by Art Joliff

00121405

Sinfonia (Arioso)
from Cantata No. 156

Bb Clarinet

J.S. Bach
Transcribed by H. Voxman

This Cantata was composed by Bach ca. 1730. The original scoring of the Sinfonia is for solo oboe, strings, and continuo. The eighth-note accompaniment figures (treble) should probably be played quasi pizzicato. Bach also used this melody in a more elaborate version in his F minor Concerto for Clavier.

00121405

Romance and Troika
from *Lieutenant Kijé*

B♭ Clarinet

Sergei Prokofiev
Arranged by Herman A. Hummel

Berceuse

Bb Clarinet

J.Ed. Barat
Edited by H. Voxman

Adagio and Allegro
from Sonata No. 6 for Violin

B♭ Clarinet

G.F. Handel
Transcribed by H. Voxman

First Concertino

B♭ Clarinet

Georges Guilhaud
Transcribed by H. Voxman

* Designates a recording "click" (accomp. recording only)

† Three fast clicks here anticipate the triplet rhythm in the piano accompaniment at *a tempo*.